MW00770857

100 - DAY

TRAUMA JOURNAL

THIS JOURNAL BELONGS TO

Day 1

List 10 things that make you happy

Day 2

Write about something someone told you about yourself that you didn't know

Day 3

Write about 5 things that win your heart

Day 4

Sharing something you struggle with

Day 5

Share some words of wisdom that speak to you

Day 6

Write about something that you feel very strongly about

Day 7

Share something that you always think "What if" about

Day 8

Write about 5 blessings in your life

Day 9

Write about something or someone that you miss

Day 10

Share the top 5 movies you love and never tire of watching

Day 11

What are three lessons you want your children/friends to learn from you

Day 12

Share some highs and lows from you month

Day 13

What are some goals you have for the next 30 days

Day 14

Write 10 words of wisdom to give your younger self.

Day 15

The greatest challenge in
my life right now is

Day 16

What are the three things that scare you the most and why?

Day 17

Do you have any recurring dreams?

Day 18

Is there anything you're scared to admit out loud?

Day 19

When was the last time you cried?

Day 20

What is your favorite way to express yourself

Day 21

What 3 things are you grateful for today?

Day 22

Do you feel about yourself today?

Day 23

List 3 things you are grateful for in life

Day 24

What's something you've been putting of lately?

Day 25

What is the most important thing you have learned about yourself in the past year?

Day 26

What do you want for your future?

Day 27

When was the last time someone made you feel special and valued?

Day 28

What do I love the most about myself?

Day 29

Make a list of goals you want to achieve in life

Day 30

What can I do to make a positive difference in my life?

Day 31

Make an emotional list of all the things that make you happy or sad

Day 32

Write about an event that made you feel sad

Day 33

Write about an event that made you feel happy

Day 34

How can you make this week a better one than last?

Day 35

Write about a childhood memory that has stuck with you

Day 36

Write down five things that make up your identity (personality traits, hobbies, etc.)

Day 37

It can be a great outlet for expressing your thoughts and feelings.

Day 38

Writing down thoughts as they come to mind helps with problem-solving

Day 39

What is something you would love to do but aren't sure you can?

Day 40

Do you have any regrets about how you've lived your life so far?

Day 41

What are your passions in life and why do you enjoy them?

Day 42

What makes you feel most fulfilled in life and why is that important to you?

Day 43

What do you want more of in your life and what do you want less of moving forward?

Day 44

If money was no object, what would be the one thing you would want to change about your life?

Day 45

What are your biggest accomplishments in life so far?

Day 46

What makes you feel most fulfilled in life?

Day 47

What do you fear most and why?

Day 48

What would you like to change about yourself and why?

Day 49

What motivates you to achieve your goals?

Day 50

Describe your safe space

Day 51

Five things for which I am grateful

Day 52

Write a letter of self-compassion about something that makes me insecure or shameful

Day 53

What are my important values?

Day 54

How am I feeling right now? How does this make me behave?

Day 55

What are my top positive self-statements?

Day 56

Who are the most important people in my life and why?

Day 57

Write my bucket list

Day 58

What are your top 5 priorities?

Day 59

What are you good at?

Day 60

What fear have you overcome?

Day 61

What are you thankful for?

Day 62

What do I need less of in my life?

Day 63

What do I need more of in my life?

Day 64

What would you like to learn?

Day 65

What is your best childhood memory?

Day 66

What would you tell your future self?

Day 67

What would you tell your past self?

Day 68

What are your favorite hobbies and why?

Day 69

What qualities do you admire most?

Day 70

What do I need to get off my chest today?

Day 71

What calms me down after a difficult day?

Day 72

How are you feeling... really?

Day 73

What does success mean to you?

Day 74

List 25 things you're grateful to know.

Day 75

Write out 5 positive affirmations for self-love.

Day 76

What are your favorite color combinations?

Day 77

What are your favorite animals?

Day 78

List 15 inspiring people

Day 79

What good advice would your future self give you

Day 80

Describe some valuable lessons you've learned in life.

Day 81

List 10 things you'd like to share with the world.

Day 82

Describe a fun day at the park.

Day 83

What is your perfect night routine?

Day 84

List your top favorite movies from your childhood

Day 85

Describe your ideal camping trip

Day 86

What food are you serving at your ideal BBQ?

Day 87

Write about your goals for the next 6 months.

Day 88

Where would you like to live?

Day 89

Who do you think you were in a past life?

Day 90

What are you passionate about?

Day 91

What do you want to achieve in your career or work life?

Day 92

List 5 ways you can bring more happiness to your daily routine.

Day 93

What "wow's you" the most about life?

Day 94

List 5 current trends and how you feel about them

Day 95

Describe your ideal city vacation

Day 96

What are your goals for this week?

Day 97

List a few ways you could improve your daily routine.

Day 98

Describe your ideal date night.

Day 99

List 10 relaxing activities for de-stressing

Day 100

What are your favorite time periods from history?

Notes

Notes

Notes

Notes

Notes

Notes

Notes

Notes

Made in the USA
Coppell, TX
21 September 2023

21838715R00066